Usborne Bible Tales

JOSEPH
AND HIS
AMAZING COAT

Retold by Heather Amery

Illustrated by Norman Young
Designed by Maria Wheatley

Language consultant: Betty Root
Series editor: Jenny Tyler

This is Joseph with Jacob, his father.

Joseph had eleven brothers. Benjamin was the youngest. They lived in Canaan long ago.

Jacob loved Joseph best.

He gave Joseph a wonderful coat. Joseph's brothers were very jealous and hated him.

Joseph looked splendid in his coat.

One brother said, "Let's kill him." But another said, "No, let's sell him as a slave."

The brothers put blood on Joseph's coat.

They took it home. "Father," they said, "this is Joseph's coat." Jacob thought Joseph was dead.

Joseph was taken to Egypt to be sold.

"I'll buy him," said Potiphar, captain of the King's guard. "He can run my house for me."

Potiphar's wife made trouble for Joseph.

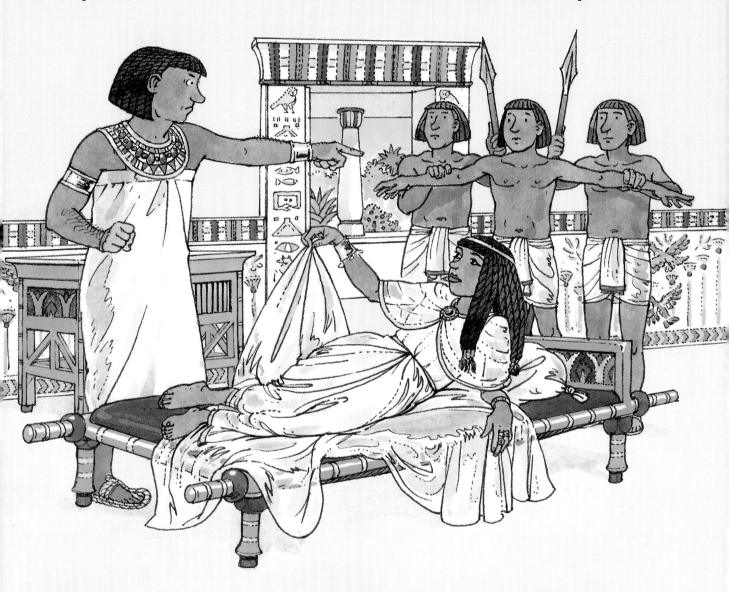

"He's rude to me," she said. It was not true, but Potiphar had Joseph put in prison.

The King had a strange dream.

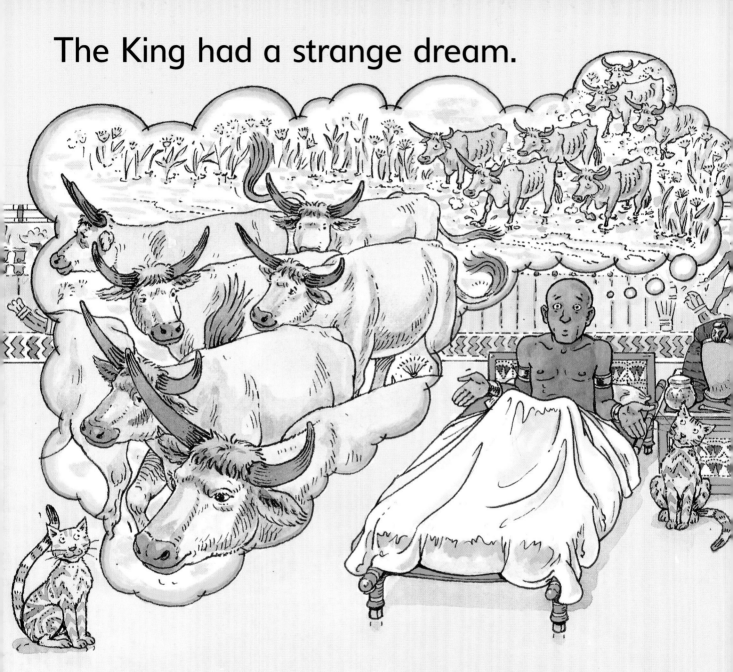

He dreamed that seven fat cows came out of the Nile. Then seven very thin cows came out.

"What does it mean?" said the King.

The King's wise men and priests did not know. One said, "Joseph is good at telling what dreams mean."

"Bring Joseph here," said the King.

"Your dream means good harvests for seven years. Then seven bad years," said Joseph.

Joseph was put in charge of harvests.

During the seven good years, he stored lots of food away. Then the seven bad, hungry years came.

Jacob sent his sons to buy food.

Joseph saw them. "They are my brothers," he thought, "but they don't know who I am."

The brothers took the food home.

On the way, guards stopped them. In a sack they found a gold cup. Joseph had hidden it there.

The brothers were taken to Joseph.

"You may go home, but you must leave your brother, Benjamin, here with me," said Joseph.

"Please keep us."

"Let Benjamin go home or it will break our father's heart," the brothers said.

Joseph saw his brothers had changed.

"I am your brother Joseph," he said. "Send for our father and we will all live well in Egypt."

This edition first published in 2003 by Usborne Publishing Ltd, 83-85 Saffron Hill, London EC1N 8RT, England. www.usborne.com
Copyright © 2003, 1997 Usborne Publishing Ltd.